Junior Library of Money

UNDERSTANDING THE STOCK MARKET

by Helen Thompson

36.84

1.56   65.36   -1.58   6.36   20.58   78.20

-1.20   45.36   -3.21   32.58   72.24   54.89

7.23   41.63

64.23   65.81

19.55   43.57   25.67

84.20   88.69

88.60   2.36

0,000

,500

00

-509.39

-687.91

Day's loss: -369.88

9:30A.M.   NooN   9:30A.M.   NooN

NooN

+35

MASON CREST PUBLISHERS INC.
370 Reed Road
Broomall, Pennsylvania 19008
(866)MCP-BOOK (toll free)
www.masoncrest.com

First Printing
9 8 7 6 5 4 3 2 1

Library of Congress Cataloging-in-Publication Data
Thompson, Helen, 1957–
Understanding the stock market / by Helen Thompson.
      p. cm.
Includes bibliographical references and index.
ISBN 978-1-4222-1773-3 (hbk.)   ISBN 978-1-4222-1759-7 (series)
ISBN 978-1-4222-1892-1 (pbk.)   ISBN 978-1-4222-1878-5 (pbk. series)
1. Stock exchanges—United States—Juvenile literature. 2. Stocks—United States—Juvenile literature. 3. Investments—United States—Juvenile literature. I. Title.
HG4553.T46 2011
332.64'273—dc22
                                    2010028431

Design by Wendy Arakawa.
Produced by Harding House Publishing Service, Inc.
www.hardinghousepages.com
Cover design by Torque Advertising and Design.
Printed by Bang Printing.

Contents

Introduction

Our lives interact with the global financial system on an almost daily basis: we take money out of an ATM machine, we use a credit card to go shopping at the mall, we write a check to pay the rent, we apply for a loan to buy a new car, we set something aside in a savings account, we hear on the evening news whether the stock market went up or down. These interactions are not just frequent, they are consequential. Deciding whether to attend college, buying a house, or saving enough for retirement, are decisions with large financial implications for almost every household. Even small decisions like using a debit or a credit card become large when made repeatedly over time.

And yet, many people do not understand how to make good financial decisions. They do not understand how inflation works or why it matters. They do not understand the long-run costs of using consumer credit. They do not understand how to assess whether attending college makes sense, or whether or how much money they should borrow to do so. They do not understand the many different ways there are to save and invest their money and which investments make the most sense for them.

And because they do not understand, they make mistakes. They run up balances they cannot afford to repay on their credit card. They drop out of high school and end up unemployed or trying to make ends meet on a minimum wage job, or they borrow so much to pay for college that they are drowning in debt when they graduate. They don't save enough. They pay high interests rates and fees when lower cost options are available. They don't buy insurance to protect themselves from financial risks. They find themselves declaring bankruptcy, with their homes in foreclosure.

We can do better. We must do better. In an increasingly sophisticated financial world, everyone needs a basic knowledge of our financial system. The books in this series provide just such a foundation. The series has individual books devoted specifically to the financial decisions most relevant to children: work, school, and spending money. Other books in the series introduce students to the key institutions of our financial system: money, banks, the stock market, the Federal Reserve, the FDIC. Collectively they teach basic financial concepts: inflation, interest rates, compounding, risk vs. reward, credit ratings, stock ownership, capitalism. They explain how basic financial transactions work: how to write a check, how to balance a checking account, what it means to borrow money. And they provide a brief history of our financial system, tracing how we got where we are today.

There are benefits to all of us of having today's children more financially literate. First, if we can help the students of today start making wise financial choices when they are young, they can hopefully avoid the financial mishaps that have been so much in the news of late. Second, as the financial crisis of 2007–2010 has shown, poor individual financial choices can sometimes have implications for the health of the overall financial system, something that affects everyone. Finally, the financial system is an important part of our overall economy. The students of today are the business and political leaders of tomorrow. We need financially literate citizens to choose the leaders who will guide our economy through the inevitable changes that lie ahead.

Brigitte Madrian, Ph.D.
Aetna Professor of Public Policy
and Corporate Management
Harvard Kennedy School

WHAT IS THE STOCK MARKET?

The stock market is the term people use to talk about the network where stocks and bonds are "traded." This means that shares in companies are bought and sold. The goal is to buy the stock, hold it for a time, and then sell the stock for more than you paid for it. It's a way of investing money—in other words, a way to make money from your money.

Investing is different from saving. When you save money, you set it aside for something you'll need in the future. You can get to your money whenever you need it, and there's no risk that you will end up with less money than you started out with. But when you invest money in something like the stock market, you can't pull that money out as easily. You also run the risk of losing some—or even all—of your money if the value of the stocks and bonds you bought goes down. The higher the risk, the greater the chances of a higher return.

Investing in the stock market is never a sure thing. You could earn a lot of money. But you could also lose money. So before you start buying and selling stocks, it's important to understand as much about the stock market as you can.

WHAT ARE $TOCKS?

Imagine a company named Wonderful Widgets. Wonderful Widgets makes wonderful widgets (obviously), and the company has grown to the point that it's worth several million dollars. The owners of the company decide to "go public." This means they're going to sell shares of the company to the public (people like you and me).

A share of stock is the smallest unit of ownership in a company. Imagine that Wonderful Widgets is a pie that's been cut into pieces. Each piece is a share of the pie. If you were to buy shares of Wonderful Widget's stock, you would now be a part owner of the company.

This means you now have the right to vote on members of the board of directors and other important matters having to do with Wonderful Widgets. If the company distributes profits to shareholders, you will receive a **proportionate** share.

One of the unique features of stock ownership is the notion of limited liability. If the company loses a lawsuit and must pay a huge judgment, the worst that can happen is your stock becomes worthless. The creditors can't come after your personal **assets**.

If you want, you can turn around and sell the shares you bought in Wonderful Widgets. But the price you get for your shares may not be the same as it was when you bought them. If Wonderful Widgets has continued to do well and make money, your shares will be worth even more than they were when you first purchased them—so you will make a profit on their sale. But if Wonderful Widgets is no longer doing so well, you may take a loss when you sell your shares.

Determining the Value of Stocks

Let's say that you want to start your own business. You decide to open a lemonade stand, so you build the stand, buy the lemons, purchase glasses and pitchers, and hire one of your friends to help you. Then you advertise (you put up a sign by the road), and you're ready for business. Altogether, you spent $25 for all the materials you needed to go into business.

You run your lemonade stand for a full month. In that first month, you spent another $10 on supplies and payroll. When you add up all the money you received from customers, you find that you brought in $105. So, since you made $105 and paid out $35, your profit is:

$$\$105 \text{ (income)} - \$25 \text{ (starting costs)} - \$10 \text{ (expenses)} = \$70 \text{ (profit)}$$

You decide to keep the lemonade stand going for another month. At the end of the second month, you've brought in $135 and your regular expenses remained the same ($10), so this month your profit is $125. At this point, you decide you're tired of running a lemonade stand and you want to sell the business. What is it worth?

One way to look at it is to say that the business is worth $25, the original amount you spent. If you close the lemonade stand, you can sell it, the equipment, and everything else and get $25. This is the asset value, or book value, of the business, the value of all of the business's assets if you sold them outright today. But your lemonade stand is really worth more than that, because if you kept the stand going, it would probably make at least another $125 next month, based on its history. Looking at it that way, someone might be willing to pay $125 for the stand because of what the stand will most likely earn next month. So if you think of the lemonade stand as a "business pie," the entire pie is worth $125—and now you can start to cut up that pie.

Selling Shares

Now, let's say 10 people come to you and say, "I would like to buy your lemonade stand but I don't have $125."

You might want to somehow divide your lemonade business—your "pie"—into 10 equal pieces and sell each piece for $12.50. In other words, you might sell shares in the lemonade stand.

= $125

1/10 = $12.⁵⁰

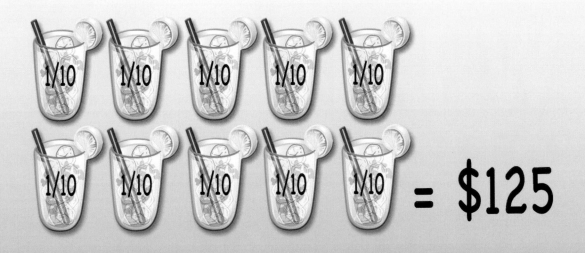 = $125

You can't cut the actual lemonade stand into 10 pieces, of course, but can divide up the profits. So each person who bought a share would receive one-tenth of the profits ($12.50 each month if the lemonade stand continues to make $125), and each person would have one out of 10 votes in any business decisions.

Or, instead, you might divide ownership up into 100 shares and sell each share for $1.25 to make the price something that even more people could afford. In this case, some people might want to buy one share, but others might want to buy 5 shares or 10 or even more.

You might decide you want to keep 55 shares for youself, and only sell 45. This would mean that you keep a majority of the shares (and therefore, you'll have a majority of the votes) and remain in control of the lemonade stand while sharing the profits with other people.

WHAT ARE DIVIDENDS?

Each of the shareholders in your lemonade stand business will receive dividends. In a real business, these would normally be paid once a year. A dividend on a share of stock is that share's portion of the company's profits.

So if your lemonade stand has 10 owners, each owning one share of stock, and the stand makes $1500 in profit during the year ($125 a month), then each owner gets a dividend of $150 at the end of the year.

Let's say eventually your lemonade stand makes $1.5 million a year. (There's a HUGE demand for lemonade!) In that case, if there are still only 10 shareholders, the total profits of the company are divided by 10 and sent to the shareholders as dividends—and each person would get $150,000. In real life, though, a company that big would probably have thousands of shareholders.

WHAT IS A CORPORATION?

Any business that wants to sell shares of stock does so by turning itself into a corporation. The process of turning a business into a corporation is called incorporating.

So if you used only your own money to build your lemonade stand, then what you started out with is called a sole proprietorship. You own the entire lemonade stand yourself.

You get to make all of the decisions and you keep all the profit. If, on the other hand, you and two other people were to pool your money together and start a lemonade stand as a team, what you have done is formed a partnership. All of you own the stand, and you share the profit and decision-making.

But a corporation is different. A corporation is a "legal person."

A corporation is registered with the government. It has a federal tax ID number, it can own property, it can go to court to sue people, it can be sued, and it can make contracts. By definition, a corporation has stock that can be bought and sold, and all the owners of the corporation hold shares of stock in the corporation. This "legal person" can also live forever, if need be!

Each corporation has a board of directors (if all the shares of a corporation are owned by one person, then that one person can decide that there will only be one person on the board of directors, but there is still a board). The shareholders in the company meet every year to vote on the people for the board. The board of directors makes the decisions for the company. It hires the officers (the president, the vice president, the secretary, and the treasurer of the company). You might say the board of directors is the brain of the "legal person." It's the part that tells the corporation how to act and what to do.

SHAREHOLDERS

A corporation has a group of owners—the shareholders. They become owners by buying shares of stock in the corporation. The board of directors decides how many total shares there will be. For example, a company might have one million shares of stock, which means that's how many shares could be sold.

A corporation can either be privately held or publicly held. In a privately held company, the shares of stock are owned by a small number of people who probably all know each other. They buy and sell their shares among themselves. A publicly held company is owned by thousands of people who trade their shares on a public stock exchange.

When a corporation first sells stock to the public, it does so in an Initial Public Offering. Selling shares is a way for the company to raise money to help the company grow (by hiring employees or buying more equipment, for example).

STOCK PRICES

Say you sell a million shares in your lemonade stand. You invest the money in building a bigger and better lemonade stand, and at the end of a year, the lemonade stand corporation has made a million dollars. (It was a hot year, and lots of people were thirsty!) The board of directors of the company can decide to do a number of things with that $1 million:

• put it in the bank and save it for a rainy day.

• give all of the profits to its shareholders, meaning that each share would pay a dividend of $1.

100

• It could use the money to buy more equipment and hire more employees to expand the company.

Or it could pick some combination of these three options. If a company pays out most of its profits to its shareholders, it is called an income stock. If the company puts most of the money back into the business, it is called a growth stock. The price of income stock stays about the same. Shareholders get income from the company every year, but the company does not grow. With a growth company, however, the shareholders don't get as many dividends, but the value of their stock goes up. This means if they decide to sell their stock, they will make a profit.

Investors in a company want to know all this information so they can make wise decisions about buying and selling stock. The ratio between price and earnings is published for every publically owned company. An organization called the Securities and Exchange Commission (SEC) is responsible for collecting this information from corporations and then making it available to investors.

THE STOCK

If you want to sell shares of your lemonade stand company, you might tell all your
friends. You might put an ad in the newspa-
per. But then how do your investors sell the
stock when they want to?

EXCHANGE

If you grew fruit and vegetables and wanted to sell them, rather than going from door to door or trying to get all your friends to buy them, you could take them to a market (or a supermarket)—a single, convenient, one-stop location for buying and selling food.

That's what the stock market is, or the stock exchange—one big place where everyone who wants to buy and sell stocks can get together and do so. You don't actually have to go there yourself, though; a stock broker is a person who goes on your behalf to buy or sell stocks.

Because all the buying and selling happens in one place, the price of a stock can be known every second of the day. Investors can watch as a stock's price goes up and down. Investors keep track of all this carefully, so they can make decisions about when to buy or sell to make the most money.

THE
BIG STOCK
EXCHANGES

The National Association of Securities Dealers (NASDAQ) is located in New York City. It was founded in 1971.

NASDAQ was the world's first electronic stock market.

DID YOU KNOW?

Today it is the largest electronic trading market in the United States.

The New York Stock Exchange (NYSE) is in New York City. It is the oldest of the stock exchanges.

The American Stock Exchange (ASEX), founded in 1953 in New York City, merged with NYSE Euronet in 2008 and became NYSE Amex Equities.

HOW DOES THE STOCK MARKET WORK?

Buy

Sell

Every day on the news you hear about the Dow Jones Industrial Average, and other stock market averages. These tell you how companies traded on the stock market are doing in general. For example, the Dow Jones Average is simply the average value of 30 large, industrial stocks. Big companies like General Motors, Goodyear, IBM, and Exxon are the companies that make up this average.

There are more than 3,000 companies listed in the NYSE.

DID YOU KNOW?

Nearly 1.5 million shares are traded each day.

What these averages tell you is the general health of stock prices as a whole. If the economy is doing well, then the average prices of all stocks tend to go up. If the economy is not doing so good, prices as a group tend to drop. The averages reveal these tendencies in the market as a whole, and they also tell us something about the entire economy—all the jobs, products, and resources (in other words, everything that has to do with money).

WHAT'S A BULL MARKET?

When the stock market's numbers are going up, investors refer to this as a "bull market." This mean that things are going well in the economy. A person might also say, "I'm feeling bullish," meaning that she feels like making investments. She's **optimistic** and willing to take risks.

During a bull market, the prices of stocks generally go higher. The graph of the daily prices will look like the lines below, with little dips and valleys in between generally rising overall numbers. A market is said to be bullish if prices go up by at least 20 percent.

For investors, it's a win-win situation: the value of their stocks are increasing AND they're making profits (leading to higher dividend payments). Trends like these usually last from five to twenty-five years—and then the market may swing the other way.

Calling a market a "bull" refers to the way a bull defends itself, by thrusting its horns upward. Also, bulls are known for being active and aggressive.

So a bull is a metaphor for the atmosphere in a stock exchange where value is high, lots of trading is going on, and the economy is generally thriving.

WHAT'S A BEAR MARKET?

Markets plummet

Recession ahead

ossible acqu

announce

Financial news

Bankruptcies feared

off m

A bear market, on the other hand, is just the opposite of a bull market. Bears swipe downward with their paws when they fight—and in a bear market, prices drop. Bears are also slower and more sluggish than bulls.

If the market falls by more than 20 percent, people say we have entered a bear market. During a market like this, investors lose confidence. Selling goes down, and prices fall.

Some investors think you should buy stocks during a bear market, when prices are low, and sell them during a bull market, when prices go up. But it's not that simple. People's emotions play a big role in the stock market—and people tend to get scared during bear markets. They're afraid their stocks' value will drop even lower, so they sell—and this in turn, makes the prices drop still more, because so many people are trying to get rid of their stock.

The History of the Stock Market

One of the officers of the Dutch East India Company, the first company to sell shares.

In twelfth-century France, men known as the *courratiers de change* managed and regulated the debts farmers owed to banks. Because these men also traded debts back and forth, they could be called the first brokers. In the middle of the thirteenth century, bankers began to trade government loans. In 1351, the city of Venice outlawed the act of spreading rumors intended to lower the price of government funds. Other countries had also begun trading government loans during the fourteenth century.

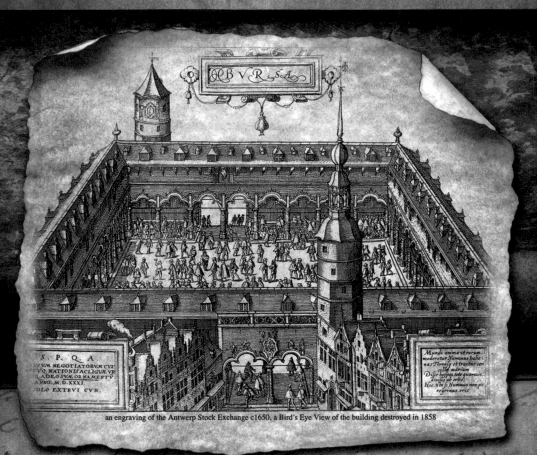

an engraving of the Antwerp Stock Exchange c1650, a Bird's Eye View of the building destroyed in 1858

The Antwerp Stock Exchange was one of the earliest to be established. Eventually, stock markets would be created in countries around the world.

The first stock exchange was formed in 1531 in Belgium, and by the late 1500s, the Dutch had joint stock companies that allowed shareholders to invest in business ventures and get a share of their profits—or the losses. In 1602, the Dutch East India Company issued the first share on the Amsterdam Stock Exchange. The same company that funded the Pilgrims' voyage to North America was also the first company to issue stocks and bonds. Investors in the Dutch East India Company received an 18 percent dividend on its profits for more than two hundred years.

THE BRITISH STOCK MARKET

The London Stock Exchange is one of the oldest of the world's major stock exchanges. It can trace its history back to 1698 when London brokers began meeting in an outdoor market in Exchange Alley. In 1725, a man named John Castaing began to organize the market in Jonathan's Coffeehouse using a simple list of stock prices. In 1773, the coffeehouse was renamed "the Stock Exchange."

An advertisement from the 1700s by a broker named John Taylor proclaimed:

Buyeth and selleth new lottery tickets,
Navy victualling bills,
East India bonds,
and other publick securities.

Today, the London Stock Exchange still exists. It is one of the biggest in the world and lists 3,500 companies from 84 different countries

The Birth of the New York Stock Market

New York City, originally called New Amsterdam, started out as a small city built at the mouth of the Hudson River.

In 1792, America was a young country. New York City was its biggest city. (Its population was about 34,000, not including Brooklyn and Queens, which were still separate towns.) Wall Street was New York's center of commerce. Just a few blocks long, the street was not yet even paved. Warehouses for furs, coffee and tea, and other goods from all over the world lined the busy street, while to the south, streets were crowded with slaughterhouses and tanneries (places for making leather). Wealthy businessmen would gather on Wall Street to sell lottery tickets, bonds, and shares of stocks in new banks that were forming. The hottest trading was in treasury bonds issued by the new Bank of the United States. Until 1792, a person wishing to buy or sell an investment would either advertise or spread the word among friends. Some of the first merchants to keep a supply of stock shares on hand were Leonard Bleeker at 16 Wall Street and Sutton & Harry at 20 Wall Street. The first organized stock exchange was created in 1792, under a buttonwood tree in Castle Garden (now called Battery Park). From then on, at 22 Wall Street, stocks were auctioned every day beginning at noon, sold to the highest bidder. The seller paid the exchange a commission on each stock sold. They originally called this organization The Stock Exchange Office. It was a very exclusive organization, allowing only the elite of New York's financial community to join. No women were allowed!

By the 1800s, Wall Street was a busy center for many kinds of business dealings.

The Growth of the American Stock Market

One of the largest New York organizations to compete with the New York Stock Exchange (NYSE) was a group of dealers who did business outside, rain or shine: the Curbstone Brokers. These brokers were willing to deal with stocks of smaller companies that couldn't meet the requirements to be listed on NYSE's "Big Board." Using prices set earlier in the day at the NYSE, the Curbstone Bankers would gather in the evenings to auction as little as a single share at a time. (NYSE set a minimum limit of 100 shares.) After more than a hundred years, the Curbstone Brokers decided it was time to move inside. In 1919, they built a building on Wall Street. (Later, in 1953, they changed their name to the American Stock Exchange.) During the 1800s, business at both stock exchanges was roaring!

THE GREAT STOCK MARKET CRASH

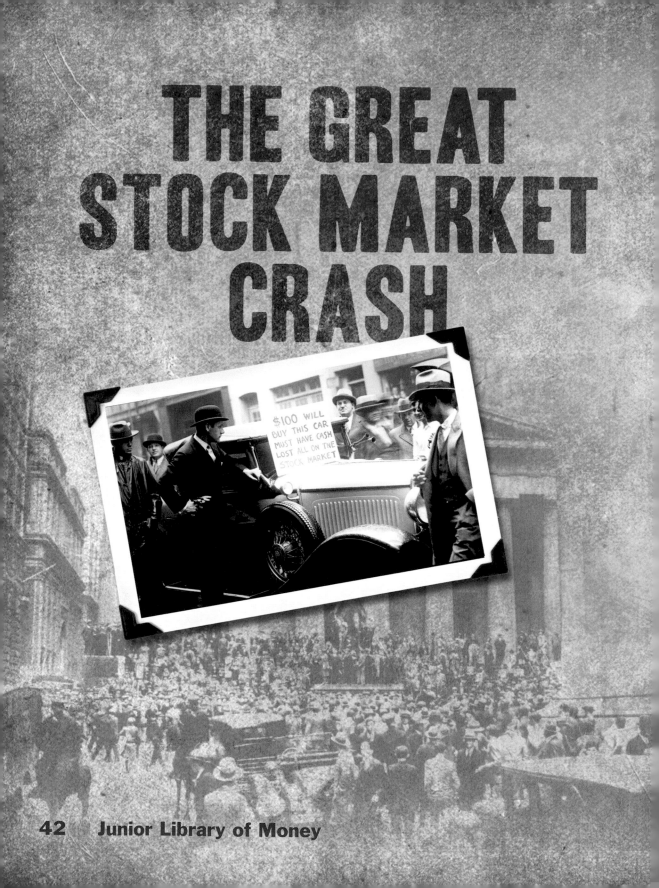

At the beginning of the twentieth century, businesses were doing great in America. The stock market was definitely bullish. And then suddenly, in 1929, the bottom dropped out. The stock market plunged lower and lower. Banks failed. Businessmen lost their investments. The bull was gone from the stock market—and a big, ugly bear was in its place. What came to be known as the "Great Stock Market Crash" was the beginning of a **depression** that changed the lives of all Americans. Thousands of people were without jobs, and making ends meet became a constant challenge for families across the United States.

THE MODERN STOCK MARKET

NASDAQ (left), with its focus on electronic trading, speaks of itself as the "stock market for the next 100 years."

The Bombay Stock Exchange (shown to the right, located in Mumbai, India) is the oldest stock exchange in Asia, and the third largest in the world (in terms of number of companies it lists).

The London Stock Exchange, one of the biggest and oldest in the world, did business out of this building (shown to the left) until 2004.

The Hong Kong Stock Exchange (right) is Asia's second largest stock exchange.

Tokyo's Stock Exchange (below) is the second largest stock exchange in the world (NYSE is the largest) and the largest in Asia.

Today, a person who invests in the stock market can do business all around the world. Different stock exchanges operate in most of the world's major cities. Can you guess the total value of all those stocks being traded?

More than $36 trillion!

THE STOCK MARKET & THE ECONOMY

The stock market and the economy are closely linked. When the stock market is bullish, that tends to be good for everything else that has to do with money—jobs, sales, and prices.

When the stock market doesn't do as well—when there's a bear market—the economy often suffers as well. Unemployment may rise, while inflation goes up. In other words, fewer people have jobs, but things cost more.

Understanding the Stock Market **47**

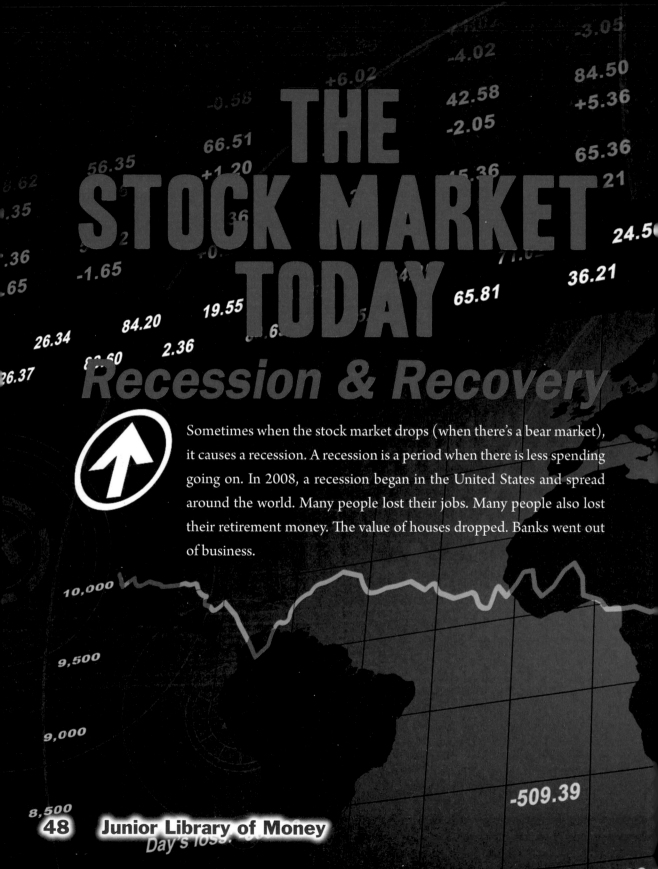

THE STOCK MARKET TODAY

Recession & Recovery

Sometimes when the stock market drops (when there's a bear market), it causes a recession. A recession is a period when there is less spending going on. In 2008, a recession began in the United States and spread around the world. Many people lost their jobs. Many people also lost their retirement money. The value of houses dropped. Banks went out of business.

-509.39

10,000

9,500

9,000

8,500

Day's loss.

9:30A

74.62
+0.63
-2.65
82.25
-5.20
30
50
65.39
68.39
-4.52
47.85
-1.58
35
-6.36
88.20
36.84
58
20.58
20.35
72.24
78.20
2.58
54.89
41.63

Governments around the world are working to bring about economic recovery. That means they are investing tax money in businesses to help them recover from the recession. As businesses get back on their feet, they can once again hire more workers—and when more people have jobs, more people spend money, which in turn is good for businesses. Getting out of a recession is complicated, and it takes awhile—but sooner or later, the bear leaves the market and the bull comes back!

-687.91

Periods of recession and recovery are cyclical. Sometimes, it takes just one thing to start the cycle. Once the cycle starts, it's hard to stop.

DID YOU KNOW?

One bad thing—or one good thing—can lead to more and more things that affect the economy.

9:30A.M.

NooN

THE STOCK MARKET AND YOU *Investing*

When you buy stock in a corporation, you own part of that company. This gives you a vote at annual shareholder meetings, and a right to a share of future profits—and it also gives you the chance to make money. Most older and larger companies pay a regular dividend to shareholders, while most newer and smaller companies do not. Newer companies would rather use their profits for research and development, expansion into new markets, and "growing" the business.

But investors buy shares because they want to make money.

So they buy stock hoping that the stock's price will go up and that the shares can be sold at a profit. This will happen if more investors want to buy stock in a company than want to sell. Investors want to buy into companies that are doing well, the ones that are selling lots of their products and making money. A company that's a leader in a hot industry (like lemonade on a hot day!) will usually see its share prices shoot up. This is good news for investors. If their stocks are worth more money, investors can sell them and make a profit.

The stock market may seem confusing, but that's mostly because it uses special words that not everyone understands. Stocks can be bought and sold by anyone who has money (even kids!). The more you understand about how the stock market works, the more likely you are to make good investments.

Most stock trading activities are done through a go-between, a broker. Brokers take orders from investors, and then the brokers buy and sell stock for the investors.

THE STOCK MARKET AND YOU
Getting Started

Some brokers can also offer investment advice to their clients. Such brokers are called full-service brokers, and they charge a higher **commission**. The types of brokers that do not offer investment advice to their clients are called discount brokers. Investors who wish to save more money usually hire discount brokers because they charge less commission.

Investors tell their brokers how much money they want to spend for stock. They also tell their brokers when they want to sell their stock, if the stock drops below a certain price. Then the brokers keep track of the rise and fall of the stocks for their clients.

If you think you're interested in investing in the stock market, you should learn more about it. Read books that explain the stock market in greater detail. Research some stocks using websites and newspapers. Before you actually spend any money, pretend you have purchased specific stocks— and then see how your investments do. If you "lose" money, try to figure out why. And if your stock does well and you "make" money, see if you can determine the factors that made a difference.

If you decide to purchase some actual stock, you can find a discount broker online. Most discount brokers will charge between $7 and $25 for each trade, so be sure to include this expense when you're deciding what to invest. Start out small! Remember, there are no guarantees in the stock market—lots of really smart investors have lost lots of money!

THE STOCK MARKET AND YOU

Dealing with Risk

Any time you invest money in the stock market, there's an element of risk involved. If that makes you uncomfortable, you may not have the right personality for the stock market!

Experts in the stock market break risk down into four general categories. You may be able to handle the level of risk at one level but not a higher level. Low risk is for people who just want to earn a litte more than they would if they had put their money in a savings account. Moderate risk is for people who can accept the possibility of losing 10% or more of their money in one year. The goal of high-risk investments is to earn above-average returns.

The greater the risk, the greater the possible profits—and the greater the possible losses as well.

People who invest in the stock market usually have careful, well-thought-out **strategies**. But to some extent, the stock market is always a gamble. There are no guarantees you'll win.

Be sure to stay within your comfort zone!
Never risk more than you can afford to lose.

HERE'S WHAT YOU NEED TO REMEMBER

- The stock market refers to how pieces of various companies are bought and sold.

- Investing money means making money from your money. It's a lot less sure than saving money—while you might earn a lot more money than you started with, you might also lose a lot of money.

- A share is a piece of the company that you can buy. Each person who owns one of these shares receives dividends each year, or a portion of that company's profits.

- A corporation is any business that splits itself into different shares. In many ways, it has the same legal rights as a person; it pays taxes, can sue or be sued, can own property, or make contracts. It is run by a board of directors that makes decisions for the company.

- The Dow Jones Industrial Average is a measure of how thirty large stocks are doing. It serves as a measure for the strength of the rest of the stock market as well.

- A "bull-market" means a time when the stock market is doing well and the values of shares are doing well, while a "bear-market" is the opposite.

- The stock market and the economy are connected; when one is doing well, so is the other.

Words You Need to Know

assets: Any item of economic value owned by an individual or corporation, especially if it has a cash value.

commission: A fee charged by a broker or agent for his or her services, such as the buying or selling of stocks.

depression: A long-term downturn in economic activities, more severe than a recession. The Great Depression of the 1930s is considered to have begun with the stock market crash of 1929.

inflation: The tendency of prices for goods and services in an economy to rise over time, causing the "value" (the buying power) of money to fall.

optimistic: Having a positive feeling about the future.

proportionate: In an amount that is fair and balanced.

strategies: Well thought out plans for getting particular results.

Further Reading

Gardner, David, Tom Gardner, and Selena Maranjian. *The Motley Fool Investment Guide for Teens: 8 Steps to Having More Money Than Your Parents Ever Dreamed Of*. New York: The Motley Fool, Inc., 2002.

Godin, Seth. *If You're Clueless About the Stock Market and Want to Know More*. Chicago, Ill.: Dearborn Trade, 2001.

Hirsch, Jeffrey A. *Stock Trader's Almanac 2010* (Almanac Investor Series). Hoboken, N.J.: John Wiley & Sons, 2010.

Karlitz, Gail. *Growing Money: A Complete Investing Guide for Kids*. New York: Price Stearn Sloane, 2001.

O'Neil, William. *How to Make Money in Stocks: A Winning System in Good Times and Bad*, Fourth Edition. New York: McGraw Hill Companies, 2009.

Orr, Tamra. *A Kid's Guide to Stock Market Investing*. Hockessin, Del.: Mitchell Lane Publishers, 2009.

Find Out More on the Internet

CNN Money News
money.cnn.com/data/us_markets

Google Finance
www.google.com/finance

Market Watch
www.marketwatch.com

The NASDAQ website
www.nasdaq.com

New York Stock Exchange
www.nyse.com

The websites listed on this page were active at the time of publication. The publisher is not responsible for websites that have changed their address or discontinued operation since the date of publication. The publisher will review and update the websites upon each reprint.

Index

Photo Credits

Alex Hinds; pp. 54–55

Amsterdams Historisch Museum; pp. 34–35

Christian Ferrari; pp. 22–23

Creative Commons: pp. 36–37, 44–45
Massimo Catarinella; pp. 26–27
Ryan Lawler; pp. 8–9

Dreamstime:
Ahmed Aboul-seoud; pp. 24–25
Carman; pp. 12–13

Dimensions Design; pp. 14–15

Gino Santa Maria; pp. 32–33

Gualtiero Boffi; pp. 16–17

Jennbang; pp. 48–49

Jiří Kábele; pp. 50–51

Madartists; pp. 10–11, 22–23

Marek Slusarczyk; pp. 32–33

Modest777; pp. 12–13

Omnibus; pp. 26–27

Photobee; pp. 52–53

Reckoning; pp. 46–47

Rolfimages; pp. 20–21

SpectrumInfo; pp. 50–51

Xetra; pp. 30–31

Granger Collection; pp. 42–43

Marco Silva; pp. 30–31

Marc Slingerland; pp. 24–25

Musée des Beaux-Arts, Grenoble; pp. 34–35

The NASDAQ OMZ Group, Inc.; pp. 8–9, 26–27, 44–45

New York State Museum; pp. 38–39, 40–41

Nick Benjaminsz; pp. 28–29

PD; pp. 36–37, 38–39, 42–43

Sergio Roberto Bichara; pp. 20–21

Summersky; pp. 54–55

Svilen Milev; pp. 18–19, 28–29

About the Author and Consultant

Helen Thompson lives in upstate New York. She worked first as a social worker and then became a teacher as her second career. She taught money management skills to students in grades seven and eight for several years.

Brigitte Madrian is Professor of Public Policy and Corporate Management in the Aetna Chair at Harvard University's Kennedy School of Government. She has also been on the faculty at the Wharton School and the University of Chicago. She is also a Research Associate at the National Bureau of Economic Research and coeditor of the *Journal of Human Resources*. She is the first-place recipient of the National Academy of Social Insurance Dissertation Prize and the TIAA-CREF Paul A. Samuelson Award for Scholarly Research on Lifelong Financial Security.